# cakes
## and cookies

TRIDENT PRESS INTERNATIONAL

*Published by:*
*TRIDENT PRESS INTERNATIONAL*
*801 12th Avenue South*
*Suite 302*
*Naples, FL 34102 U.S.A.*
*Copyright (c)Trident Press International 2001*
*Tel: (941) 649 7077*
*Fax: (941) 649 5832*
*Email: tridentpress@worldnet.att.net*
*Website: www.trident-international.com*

# acknowledgements

*Cakes & Cookies*

*Compiled by: R&R Publications Marketing P/L*
*Creative Director: Paul Sims*
*Production Manager: Anthony Carroll*
*Food Photography: Warren Webb,*
*Andrew Elton, Quentin Bacon, Per Ericson,*
*Paul Grater, Ray Joice, John Stewart,*
*Ashley Mackevicius, Harm Mol,*
*Yanto Noerianto, Andy Payne.*
*Food Stylists: Wendy Berecry,*
*Michelle Gorry, Donna Hay.*
*Recipe Development: Ellen Argyriou,*
*Sheryle Eastwood, Lucy Kelly, Donna Hay,*
*Anneka Mitchell, Penelope Peel,*
*Jody Vassallo, Loukie Werle.*
*Proof Reader: Samantha Calcott*

*Includes Index*
*ISBN 1582791597*
*EAN 9781582791593*

*First Edition Printed June 2001*
*Computer Typeset in Humanist 521*
*& Times New Roman*

*Printed in Hong Kong*

# Contents

**Introduction**
4

**Baking secrets**
5

**Chocolate**
8

**Coconut & coffee**
20

**Fruit, nuts & spice**
32

**Citrus flavours**
50

**Something savoury**
62

**Healthy alternative**
68

**Icing on the cake**
76

**Weights and measures**
78

**Index**
80

# introduction

### Baking Secrets

What happens when you make the cake? This section answers this question and many more. One of the secrets tp producing wonderful cakes and cookies is to understand why certain techniques are used.

### Making the cake

- Many recipes begin by creaming the butter and sugar. This is an important process as little bubbles of air are trapped in the mixture and it is this air which helps to produce a light-textured cake.

- The butter should be softened for the creaming process and the mixture beaten until it is creamy and fluffy and almost doubled in volume.

- Creaming can be done with a balloon whisk, wooden spoon, electric beater or a food processor.

- After the creaming process an egg or eggs are often added to the mixture. The egg white forms a layer around each bubble of air and as the cake cooks the egg white coagulates and forms a wall around each bubble, preventing the bubbles from bursting and so ruining the cake.

- As the cake cooks, the air bubbles expand and the cake rises.

- As the air bubbles are expanding, the gluten in the flour is also stretching. This will continue until the gluten loses its elasticity.

- Do not open the oven door until at least halfway through the recommended cooking time or the rising process is interrupted. With the sudden drop in temperature the cake stops expanding and it sinks because there is no structure to support it

- The oven should be preheated to the correct temperature before placing the cake in to cook.

- If baking more than one cake, arrange the tins so that they do not touch each other or the sides of the oven.

- Filling the cake tin is an important step towards a successful result. If your batter is soft it can be poured into the cake tin, however a firm batter should be spooned into the tin and spread out evenly using a spatula. For light batters, only half to two-thirds fill the tin; heavy batters can fill as much as three-quarters of the tin.

# baking
## secrets

### Is the cake cooked?

- Test the cake just before the end of the recommended cooking time. To test the cake, insert a skewer into the thickest part of the cake. If it comes away clean, your cake is cooked. If there is still cake mixture on the skewer, cook for 5 minutes longer then test again.

- Alternatively, gently press the top of the cake with your fingertips. When cooked, the depression will spring back quickly.

- When the cake starts to leave the side of the tin this is another indication that the cake is cooked.

### Cooling the cake

- You will find that a freshly baked cake is very fragile. Allow a cake to cool for a short time in the tin before turning onto a wire rack to cool completely.

- Before turning out a cake, loosen the sides with a spatula or palette knife. Then turn the cake onto a wire rack to cool and immediately invert on to a second wire rack so that the top of the cake is not marked with indentations from the rack. If you do not have a second wire rack, invert the cake onto a clean cloth on your hand then turn it back onto the wire rack.

### Storing baked products

- Allow cakes to cool completely before placing in an airtight container, or condensation will accumulate in the container and cause the cake to go mouldy.

- Keeping times for cakes vary depending on the ingredients used. A fatless sponge will only stay fresh for 1-2 days while one made with fat will keep fresh for 2-3 weeks and heavy rich fruit cakes will store for a month or more.

- Most undecorated cakes can be frozen successfully. Wrap the cake in freezer wrap or place in a freezer bag and seal. If freezing several cakes, wrap each separately or place freezer wrap or waxed paper between cakes so that they are easy to remove.

- To thaw a frozen cake, leave in package and thaw at room temperature. Large cakes will take 3-4 hours to thaw, layer cakes 1-2 hours and smaller cakes about 30 minutes.

# baking
## secrets

### Preparing the **cake tins**

To grease and flour a cake tin: using a pastry brush lightly brush cake tin with melted butter or margarine, then sprinkle with flour and shake to coat evenly. Invert tin on work surface and tap gently to remove excess flour.

To grease and line a round cake tin: Place cake tin on a large piece of baking paper and using a pencil trace around the base, then cut out a shape. Grease tin and line with paper.

To line a deep cake tin: A deep cake tine should be lined on the bottom and sides. Use a double thickness folded strip of baking paper 5cm/2in higher than the cake tin and long enough to fit around the tin and to overlap by about 2¹/₂cm/ Iin. On the folded edge turn up about 2¹/₂cm/ Iin and crease, then using scissors snip at regular intervals across the margin as far as the fold. Cut out a piece of baking paper to line the base of the tin previously. Grease the tin and place the strip inside the tin with the snipped margin lying flat on the base of the tin. Ensure that the ends overlap so that the sides are completely covered by the paper.

Place the base piece of baking paper in the tin to cover the snipped margin.

**To line a loaf tin:** Cut a strip a baking paper the width of the base of the tin and long enough to come up the shorter sides of the tin and overlap by 2¹/₂cm/Iin. Grease the tin and line with the paper. When the cake is cooked the unlined sides can be loosened with a knife and tha paper ends are used to lift out the cake.

*double choc cookies and*
*quick nut fudge cake*

# chocolate

## For many, chocolate is a delicious

*obsession. For the Aztecs, who discovered it, chocolate was 'food for the gods'. In its various forms - block chocolate, cocoa powder and chocolate chips, grated, melted and chopped - chocolate is one of the most popular ingredients in cakes, biscuits and slices.*

# double
## choc cookies

*Photograph page 9*

**ingredients**

75g/2¹/₂oz butter, softened
¹/₄ cup/60g/2oz caster sugar
1¹/₂ cups/155g/5oz flour
¹/₄ cup/30g/1oz self-raising flour
2 eggs
200g/6¹/₂oz milk chocolate,
melted and cooled
185g/6oz chocolate chips

**Method:**
1 Place butter and sugar in a food processor and process until mixture is creamy. Add flour and self-raising flour, eggs and melted chocolate and process until smooth. Stir in chocolate chips.
2 Place spoonfuls of mixture on greased baking trays and bake for 8-10 minutes or until just firm. Stand on trays for 5 minutes before transferring to wire racks to cool completely.
**Note:** An old-time favourite. Served with a glass of icy cold milk, what better treat is there.
**Makes 30**

Oven temperature 180°C, 350°F, Gas 4

# quick nut
## fudge cake

*Photograph page 9*

**ingredients**

125g/4oz butter, melted
1¹/₂ cups/250g/8oz soft brown sugar
2 eggs, lightly beaten
1 teaspoon vanilla essence
¹/₄ cup/30g/1oz cocoa powder, sifted
2 cups/250g/8oz self-raising flour, sifted
60g/2oz chopped walnuts

**Chocolate butter icing**
125g/4oz butter, softened
100g/3¹/₂oz dark chocolate,
melted and cooled
2 egg yolks
¹/₂ cup/75g/2¹/₂oz icing sugar, sifted

**Method:**
1 Place butter, brown sugar, eggs and vanilla essence in a large mixing bowl and mix to combine. Stir in cocoa powder, flour and walnuts. Mix well to combine.
2 Spoon batter into a greased and lined 20cm/8in round cake tin and bake for 35-40 minutes or until cake is cooked when tested with a skewer. Stand cake in tin for 5 minutes before turning onto a wire rack to cool.
3 To make icing, place butter in a mixing bowl and beat until light and fluffy. Add chocolate, egg yolks and icing sugar and beat until smooth. Spread icing over cold cake.
**Makes a 20cm/8in
round cake**

Oven temperature 180°C, 350°F, Gas 4

# chocolate
## sandwich cake

**Method:**

1 Place flour, bicarbonate of soda, cocoa powder, butter, sugar, eggs and sour cream in a large mixing bowl and beat until well combined and mixture is smooth.

2 Spoon batter into two greased and lined 20cm/8in sandwich tins and bake for 25-30 minutes or until cooked when tested with a skewer. Stand cakes in tins for 5 minutes before turning onto a wire rack to cool.

3 Sandwich cold cakes together with whipped cream.

4 To make icing, place chocolate and butter in a small saucepan and cook over a low heat, stirring constantly, until melted. Cool slightly then spread over top of cake.

**Makes a 20cm/8in sandwich cake**

### ingredients

1 cup/125g/4oz self-raising flour, sifted
¹/₄ teaspoon bicarbonate of soda
¹/₂ cup/45g/1 ¹/₂oz cocoa powder, sifted
125g/4oz butter, softened
³/₄ cup/170g/5¹/₂oz caster sugar
2 eggs, lightly beaten
1 cup/250g/8oz sour cream
¹/₂ cup/125mL/4fl oz cream (double), whipped

**Chocolate icing**
60g/2oz dark chocolate, chopped
30g/1oz unsalted butter

# chocolate
## shortbread

*Photograph page 13*

### ingredients

**250g/8oz butter, softened**
**1/2 cup/75g/2 1/2oz icing sugar**
**1 cup/125g/4oz flour**
**1 cup/125g/4oz cornflour**
**1/4 cup/30g/1oz cocoa powder**

**Method:**
1 *Place butter and icing sugar in a mixing bowl and beat until mixture is creamy. Sift together flour, cornflour and cocoa powder. Stir flour mixture into butter mixture.*
2 *Turn dough onto a floured surface and knead lightly until smooth. Roll spoonfuls of mixture into balls, place on greased baking trays and flatten slightly with a fork. Bake for 20-25 minutes or until firm. Allow to cool on trays.*
**Makes 30**

**Oven temperature 160°C, 325°F, Gas 3**

# brownies

*Photograph page 13*

### ingredients

**155g/5oz butter, softened**
**1/2 cup/170g/5 1/2oz honey, warmed**
**2 eggs, lightly beaten**
**1 3/4 cups/220g/7oz self-raising flour, sifted**
**2/3 cup/125g/4oz soft brown sugar**
**125g/4oz dark chocolate,**
**melted and cooled**
**icing sugar**

**Method:**
1 *Place butter, honey, water, eggs, flour, sugar and chocolate in a food processor and process until ingredients are combined.*
2 *Spoon batter into a greased and lined 23cm/ 9 in square cake tin and bake for 30-35 minutes or until cooked when tested with a skewer. Stand cake in tin for 5 minutes before turning onto a wire rack to cool. Dust cold cake with icing sugar and cut into squares.*
**Makes 25**

**Oven temperature 180°C, 350°F, Gas 4**

# white choc-chip
## chocolate cake

### Method:

1 Place butter, sugar and vanilla essence in a mixing bowl and beat until mixture is creamy. Add eggs one at a time beating well after each addition.

2 Sift together flour, cocoa powder and baking powder. Fold flour mixture and milk, alternately, into butter mixture, then fold in chocolate.

3 Spoon batter into a greased and lined 23 cm/9 in round cake tin and bake for 30-35 minutes or until cooked when tested with a skewer. Stand in tin for 5 minutes before turning onto a wire rack to cool completely.

4 To make frosting, place butter in a mixing bowl and beat until light and fluffy. Add chocolate, egg yolks and icing sugar and beat until smooth. Spread frosting over top and sides of cold cake.

**Note:** A rich chocolate cake studded with white chocolate chips and topped with creamy white chocolate frosting.

**Makes a 23cm/9in round cake**

### ingredients

125g/4oz butter, softened
1 cup/220g/7oz caster sugar
1 teaspoon vanilla essence
2 eggs
1¹/₃ cups/170g/5¹/₂oz self-raising flour
¹/₄ cup/30g/1oz cocoa powder
¹/₂ teaspoon baking powder
1 cup/250mL/8fl oz milk
200g/6¹/₂oz white chocolate, chopped

<u>**White chocolate frosting**</u>
125g/4oz butter, softened
100g/3¹/₂oz white chocolate, melted and cooled
2 egg yolks
¹/₂ cup/75g/2¹/₂oz icing sugar, sifted

# chocolate
## pinwheels

**Method:**

1 Place butter, sugar and vanilla essence in a mixing bowl and beat until mixture is creamy. Add egg and beat until well combined.

2 Divide mixture into two equal portions and mix 1 cup/125g/4oz flour into one portion and remaining flour and cocoa powder into the other portion.

3 Roll out each portion between two sheets of greaseproof paper to form a 20 x 30cm/ 8 x 12in rectangle. Remove top sheet of paper from each and invert one onto the other. Roll up from longer edge to form a long roll. Wrap in plastic food wrap and refrigerate for 1 hour.

4 Cut roll into 5mm/$^1$/$_4$in slices and place on greased baking trays. Bake for 10-12 minutes or until lightly browned. Cool on wire racks.

**Cook's tip:** These are ideal last-minute biscuits. The dough can be made in advance and kept in the refrigerator until needed.

Layers of plain and chocolate dough are rolled together to make these delicious biscuits.

**Makes 30**

## ingredients

**125g/4oz butter**
**$^2$/$_3$ cup/140g/4$^1$/$_2$oz caster sugar**
**1 teaspoon vanilla essence**
**1 egg**
**1$^3$/$_4$cups/220g/7oz flour, sifted**
**$^1$/$_4$ cup/30g/1oz cocoa powder, sifted**

**Oven temperature 180°C, 350°F, Gas 4**

15

# chocolate
## date torte

**Method:**

1 *Beat egg whites until soft peaks form. Gradually add sugar and beat until dissolved. Fold in chocolate, dates and hazelnuts.*

2 *Spoon mixture into two greased and lined 23cm/9in springform pans. Bake for 40 minutes or until firm. Remove from oven and allow to cool in pans.*

3 *Spread one meringue layer with whipped cream and top with remaining layer. Decorate top with drizzled melted chocolate.*

**Serves 4**

ingredients

**6 egg whites**
**1 cup/220g caster sugar**
**200g/6¹/₂oz dark chocolate, grated**
**160g/5oz pitted dates, chopped**
**2 cups/280g chopped hazelnuts**
**1¹/₂ cups/375mL thickened cream, whipped**

**Topping**
**100g/3¹/₂oz dark chocolate, melted**

**Oven temperature 160°C**

# berry
## chocolate mud cake

**Method:**

1. Place chocolate and butter in a heatproof bowl over a saucepan of simmering water and heat, stirring, until chocolate melts and mixture is smooth. Cool slightly.
2. Beat egg yolks and caster sugar into chocolate mixture, then fold in flour.
3. Place egg whites in a separate bowl and beat until stiff peaks form. Fold egg whites and raspberries into chocolate mixture. Pour into a greased and lined 20cm/8in round cake tin and bake for 1 1/4 hours or until cooked when tested with a skewer. Turn off oven and cool cake in oven with door ajar.
4. To make coulis, place raspberries in a food processor or blender and process until puréed. Push purée through a sieve to remove seeds. Add sugar to taste. Serve cake with coulis and cream.

**Serves 10**

### ingredients

315g/10oz dark chocolate
250g/8oz butter, chopped
5 eggs, separated
2 tablespoons caster sugar
1/4 cup/30g/1oz self-raising flour, sifted
250g/8oz raspberries
whipped cream, for serving

**Raspberry coulis**
250g/8oz raspberries
sugar to taste

**Oven temperature 120°C, 250°F, Gas 1/2**

# chocolate
## rolls

*Photograph page 19*

1 Place egg yolks and sugar in a mixing bowl and beat until mixture is thick and creamy. Beat in chocolate, then fold in flour mixture.

2 Beat egg whites until stiff peaks form and fold into chocolate mixture. Pour into a greased and lined 26x32cm/10¹/₂x12³/₄in Swiss roll tin and bake for 12-15 minutes or until just firm. Turn onto a damp teatowel sprinkled with caster sugar and roll up from the short end. Set aside to cool.

3 To make filling, place chocolate and cream in a small saucepan and cook over a low heat until chocolate melts and mixture is well blended. Bring to the boil, remove from heat and set aside to cool, completely. When cold, place in a mixing bowl over ice and beat until thick and creamy.

4 Unroll cake, spread with filling and reroll. To serve, cut into slices. A chocolate roll filled with chocolate cream makes a special afternoon tea treat or dessert. Irresistibly good to eat, these spectacular cakes are easy to make. Follow these step-by-step instructions for a perfect result every time.

**Serves 8**

**5 eggs, separated**
**¹/₄ cup/60g/2oz caster sugar**
**100g/3¹/₂oz dark chocolate, melted and cooled**
**2 tablespoons self-raising flour, sifted with 2 tablespoons cocoa powder**

**Chocolate filling**
**60g/2oz dark chocolate**
**²/₃ cup/170mL/5¹/₂fl oz cream (double)**

**Oven temperature 180°C, 350°F, Gas 4**

*austrian coffee cake*

# coconut
# &
# coffee

## The fruit of a tropical palm tree,

*coconut is mostly used in its desiccated or shredded form for baking. It adds a distinctive flavour and a moistness to baked goods that usually means they keep well. Toasted or left plain it is a wonderfully easy decoration. Coffee is one of the most popular beverages, and also plays an important role as a flavouring for cakes, biscuits, slices and sweets. If you are using instant coffee powder, dissolve it first in hot water before adding to any mixture.*

# mocha
## fudge

### ingredients

500g/1 lb dark chocolate
1 cup/250mL/8fl oz sweetened
condensed milk
30g/1oz butter
3 teaspoons instant coffee

**Method:**
1 Place chocolate, condensed milk, butter and coffee in a small saucepan and cook, stirring, over a low heat until mixture is smooth. Pour fudge into an aluminium foil-lined 20cm/8in square cake tin and refrigerate for 2 hours or until set. Cut into squares.

*Note: This coffee-flavoured chocolate fudge is sure to become a family favourite.*

**Makes 30 squares**

# austrian
## coffee cake

*Photograph page 21*

### ingredients

4 eggs, separated
1/4 cup/60g/2oz caster sugar
45g/1 1/2oz ground almonds
3 teaspoons instant coffee powder
dissolved in 4 teaspoons boiling
water, cooled
1/2 teaspoon vanilla essence
1/4 cup/30g/1oz flour
chocolate-coated coffee beans
or chocolate dots
finely grated chocolate

**Coffee cream**
1 tablespoon caster sugar
1 teaspoon instant coffee powder
dissolved in 2 teaspoons boiling
water, cooled
2 tablespoons coffee-flavoured liqueur
1 cup/250mL/8fl oz cream (double), whipped

**Method:**
1 Place egg yolks and sugar in a bowl and beat until thick and creamy. Beat in almonds, coffee mixture and vanilla essence.
2 Place egg whites in a bowl and beat until stiff peaks form. Sift flour over egg yolk mixture and fold in with egg white mixture. Spoon batter into a greased and lined 20 cm/8 in springform tin and bake for 20-25 minutes or until cooked when tested with a skewer. Stand in tin for 10 minutes, before turning onto a wire rack to cool.
3 To make Coffee Cream, mix sugar, coffee mixture and liqueur into cream. Split cold cake horizontally and use a little of the Coffee Cream to sandwich halves together. Spread remaining Coffee Cream over top and sides of cake. Decorate top of cake with coffee beans or chocolate dots and grated chocolate. Chill and serve cut into slices.

**Serves 10**

**Oven temperature 180°C, 350°F, Gas 4**

# coconut cake

**Method:**

1 Place butter and vanilla essence in a mixing bowl and beat until light and fluffy. Gradually add caster sugar, beating well after each addition until mixture is creamy.

2 Beat in egg whites, one at a time. Fold flour and milk, alternately, into creamed mixture. Divide batter evenly between two greased and lined 23cm/9in sandwich tins and bake for 25-30 minutes or until cakes are cooked when tested with a skewer. Stand in tins for 5 minutes before turning onto a wire rack to cool.

3 To make frosting, place water and sugar in a saucepan and cook over a medium heat, without boiling, stirring constantly until sugar dissolves. Brush any sugar from sides of pan using a pastry brush dipped in water. Bring syrup to the boil and boil rapidly for 3-5 minutes, without stirring, or until syrup reaches the soft ball stage (115°C/239°F on a sweet thermometer). Place egg whites in a mixing bowl and beat until soft peaks form. Continue beating while pouring in syrup in a thin stream a little at a time. Continue beating until all syrup is used and frosting will stand in stiff peaks. Beat in lemon juice.

4 Spread one cake with a little frosting and sprinkle with 2 tablespoons coconut, then top with remaining cake. Spread remaining frosting over top and sides of cake and sprinkle with remaining coconut.

**Cook's tip:** This cake looks pretty when decorated with edible flowers such as violets, rose petals or borage. This light moist sponge-type cake, covered with a white frosting and topped with shredded coconut is a must for any afternoon tea.

**Makes a 23cm/9in round cake**

## ingredients

125g/4oz butter, softened
1 teaspoon vanilla essence
1 cup/220g/7oz caster sugar
3 egg whites
2 cups/250g/8oz self-raising flour, sifted
³/₄ cup/185mL/6fl oz milk
90g/3oz shredded coconut

**Fluffy frosting**
¹/₂ cup/125mL/4fl oz water
1¹/₄ cups/315g/10oz sugar
3 egg whites
1 teaspoon lemon juice

**Oven temperature 180°C, 350°F, Gas 4**

# golden
## oat cookies

*Photograph page 25*

ingredients

**1 cup/90g/3oz rolled oats**
**1 cup/125g/4oz flour, sifted**
**90g/3oz desiccated coconut**
**1 cup/250g/8oz sugar**
**4 teaspoons golden syrup, warmed**
**125g/4oz butter, melted**
**2 tablespoons boiling water**
**1 teaspoon bicarbonate of soda**

**Method:**
1 Place oats, flour, coconut and sugar in a large mixing bowl. Combine golden syrup, butter, water and bicarbonate of soda.
2 Pour golden syrup mixture into dry ingredients and mix well to combine. Place spoonfuls of mixture 3cm/1¹/₄in apart on greased baking trays and bake for 10-15 minutes or until biscuits are just firm. Stand on trays for 3 minutes before transferring to wire racks to cool.
**Note:** Golden, crunchy and delicious, these biscuits won't last long.
**Makes 30**

**Oven temperature 180°C, 350°F, Gas 4**

# lime
## and coconut cookies

*Photograph page 25*

ingredients

**125g/4oz butter, chopped**
**1 cup/170g/5¹/₂oz soft brown sugar**
**1 teaspoon vanilla essence**
**1 egg**
**1 cup/125g/4oz flour**
**¹/₂ cup/60g/2oz self-raising flour**
**1 cup/90g/3oz rolled oats**
**45g/1¹/₂oz desiccated coconut**
**2 teaspoons finely grated lime rind**
**2 tablespoons lime juice**

**Method:**
1 Place butter, sugar, vanilla essence, egg, flour and self-raising flour, rolled oats, coconut, lime rind and lime juice in a food processor and process until well combined.
2 Place heaped spoonfuls of mixture on greased baking trays and bake for 12-15 minutes or until lightly browned. Cool on wire racks.
**Note:** The tang of lime and the unique flavour and texture of coconut combine to make these wonderful cookies.
**Makes 35**

**Oven temperature 180°C, 350°F, Gas 4**

**Oven temperature 160°C, 325°F, Gas 3**

# coffee
## sandwich cake

**Method:**

1 Place butter and sugar in a food processor and process until creamy. Add eggs, flour and baking powder and process until all ingredients are combined. Spoon batter into two greased and lined 18cm/7in sandwich tins and bake for 30-35 minutes or until golden. Turn onto a wire rack to cool.

**Note:** Layers of light sponge sandwiched together with a liqueur cream and topped with a coffee icing. All this cake needs is a wonderful cup of coffee to accompany it.

**Makes an 18cm/7in sandwich cake**

### ingredients
**250g/8oz butter, softened**
**1 cup/220g/7oz caster sugar**
**6 eggs, lightly beaten**
**2 cups/250g/8oz self-raising flour, sifted**
**4 teaspoons baking powder**

**Coffee icing**
**60g/2oz butter, softened**
**³/₄ cup/125g/4oz icing sugar, sifted**
**¹/₂ teaspoon ground cinnamon**
**2 teaspoons instant coffee powder dissolved in 2 teaspoons hot water, cooled**

**Liqueur cream**
**1 tablespoon Tia Maria Liqueur**
**¹/₂ cup/125mL/4fl oz cream (double), whipped**

# sweet
## potato and coconut cake

**Method:**

1 Place butter, sugar, lime or lemon rind and cinnamon in a bowl and beat until light and fluffy. Gradually beat in egg yolks.

2 Add sweet potato and coconut and mix well. Sift together flour, self-raising flour and bicarbonate of soda. Fold flour mixture into sweet potato mixture.

3 Place egg whites in a clean bowl and beat until stiff peaks form. Fold egg whites into sweet potato mixture.

4 Spoon mixture into two greased and lined 20cm/8in round cake tins and bake for 30 minutes or until cakes are cooked when tested with a skewer. Stand cakes in tins for 5 minutes before turning onto wire racks to cool.

5 To make filling, place cream cheese, icing sugar and lime or lemon juice in a bowl and beat until smooth.

6 To assemble cake, slice each cake in half horizontally. Place one layer of cake on a serving plate and spread with one quarter of the filling. Repeat layers with remaining cake and filling finishing with a layer of filling. Decorate with coconut and candied peel.

**Makes a 20cm/8in round cake**

## ingredients

**250g/8oz butter, softened**
**³/₄ cup/185g/6oz sugar**
**2 tablespoons finely grated lime or lemon rind**
**2 teaspoons cinnamon**
**3 eggs, separated**
**250g/8oz mashed sweet potato**
**45g/1¹/₂oz desiccated coconut**
**1 cup/125g/4oz flour**
**1 cup/125g/4oz self-raising flour**
**1 teaspoon bicarbonate of soda**
**shredded coconut, toasted**
**candied lime or lemon peel**

**<u>Cream and citrus filling</u>**
**250g/8oz cream cheese, softened and chopped**
**¹/₄ cup/45g/1¹/₂oz icing sugar**
**2 tablespoons lime or lemon juice**

**Oven temperature 160°C, 325°F, Gas 3**

# coffee
## kisses

### Method:

1 Place butter and icing sugar in a large mixing bowl and beat until light and fluffy. Stir in coffee mixture and flour.

2 Spoon mixture into a piping bag fitted with a medium star nozzle and pipe 2cm/³/₄in rounds of mixture 2cm/³/₄in apart on greased baking trays. Bake for 10-12 minutes or until lightly browned. Stand on trays for 5 minutes before removing to wire racks to cool completely.

3 Join biscuits with a little melted chocolate, then dust with icing sugar.

**Makes 25**

### ingredients

**250g/8oz butter, softened**
**²/₃ cup/100g/3¹/₂oz icing sugar, sifted**
**2 teaspoons instant coffee powder**
**dissolved in 1 tablespoon hot water, cooled**
**2 cups/250g/8oz flour, sifted**
**45g/1¹/₂oz dark chocolate, melted**
**icing sugar**

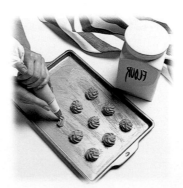

# coconut
## and raspberry cake

**Method:**

1. To make cake, place butter and sugar in a bowl and beat until light and creamy. Add egg yolks one at a time, beating well after each addition. Fold in coconut.

2. Sift flour and baking powder together. Combine vanilla essence and coconut milk. Fold flour mixture and coconut milk mixture, alternately, into butter mixture. Place egg whites in a bowl and beat until stiff peaks form. Fold egg white mixture into batter.

3. Pour batter into two greased and floured 20cm/8in square cake tins and bake for 35-40 minutes or until cake comes away from sides of tin. Stand cakes in tins for 5 minutes before turning onto wire racks to cool.

4. To assemble, top one cake with raspberries, then with remaining cake. Spread top and sides of cake with cream and sprinkle with coconut. Refrigerate until ready to serve.

5. To make coulis, place raspberries and icing sugar in a food processor or blender and process to purée. Press purée through a sieve to remove seeds. Serve with cake.

**Makes a 20cm/8in square cake**

## ingredients

200g/6¹/₂oz fresh or frozen raspberries
1¹/₂ cups/375mL/12fl oz cream (double), whipped
90g/3oz shredded coconut, toasted

### Coconut cake
185g/6oz butter, softened
1 cup/220g/7oz caster sugar
4 eggs, separated
90g/3oz desiccated coconut
3 cups/375g/12oz self-raising flour
1 teaspoon baking powder
1 teaspoon vanilla essence
³/₄ cup/185mL/6fl oz coconut milk

### Raspberry coulis
500g/1 lb fresh or frozen raspberries
2 tablespoons icing sugar

Oven temperature 180°C, 350°F, Gas 4

**Oven temperature 180°C, 350°F, Gas 4**

# coffee
## oat and date cake

### Method:

1  *To make topping, place dates, water and caster sugar in a saucepan and cook over a medium heat for 3-4 minutes or until dates are soft and mixture thickens slightly. Remove from heat and set aside to cool. Place oats, sugar and flour in a bowl and stir in butter and walnuts. Set aside.*

2  *Place butter, coffee mixture, sugar, eggs, flour and milk in a large mixing bowl and beat until all ingredients are combined and mixture is smooth. Spoon batter into a greased and lined 23cm/9in square cake tin and top with date mixture, then sprinkle over oat mixture. Bake for 40-45 minutes or until cake is cooked when tested with a skewer. Stand cake in tin for 10 minutes before turning onto a wire rack to cool.*

*Note: Sprinkled with a crunchy topping before baking this cake requires no icing.*

**Makes a 23cm/9in square cake**

### ingredients

125g/4oz butter, softened
4 teaspoons instant coffee powder
dissolved in 4 teaspoons hot water, cooled
³/₄ cup/170g/5¹/₂oz caster sugar
2 eggs, lightly beaten
1¹/₂ cups/185g/6oz self-raising flour, sifted
¹/₂ cup/125mL/4fl oz buttermilk or milk

**Date and oat topping**
200g/6¹/₂oz pitted dates, chopped
¹/₃ cup/170mL/5¹/₂fl oz water
1¹/₂ tablespoons caster sugar
3 tablespoons rolled oats
1 tablespoon soft brown sugar
2 tablespoons self-raising flour
30g/1oz butter, melted
1 tablespoon chopped walnuts

# fruit, nuts & spice

*hazelnut shortbreads and
walnut honey baklava*

## Fruit and nuts are healthy additions

to any baked product and add flavour, crunch and texture. It's usually safe to substitute your favourite fruit or nuts in a recipe and still end up with a delicious cake, biscuit or slice.

# walnut
## honey baklava

*Photograph page 33*

### ingredients

**375g/12oz filo pastry**
**155g/5oz butter, melted**

**Walnut filling**
**250g/8oz finely chopped walnuts, toasted**
**1 teaspoon ground cinnamon**
**1 teaspoon ground mixed spice**
**1/3 cup/60g/2oz soft brown sugar**

**Honey orange syrup**
**1/2 cup/125mL/4fl oz water**
**1/3 cup/90g/3oz sugar**
**1/3 cup/125g/4oz honey**
**1/3 cup/90mL/3fl oz freshly squeezed orange juice**
**2 tablespoons lemon juice**

**Method:**

1  To make filling, combine walnuts, cinnamon, mixed spice and brown sugar in a bowl and set aside.

2  Cut pastry sheets into 18 x 28cm/7 x 11in rectangles. Layer a quarter of the pastry sheets in a greased, shallow 18 x 28cm/7 x 11in cake tin, brushing each sheet with butter. Sprinkle pastry with one-third of filling, repeat with remaining pastry and filling, finish with a layer of pastry.

3  Cut pastry into squares using a sharp knife. Brush top with butter and bake for 15 minutes. Reduce oven temperature to 190°C/375°F/Gas 5 and bake for 10 minutes longer or until golden brown.

4  To make syrup, place water, sugar, honey, orange juice and lemon juice in a small saucepan and cook over a medium heat, stirring constantly, until sugar dissolves. Bring to the boil, then remove from heat and pour over hot baklava. Set aside and allow to cool completely in tin.

**Note:** The secret to this Middle Eastern specialty is to pour the hot syrup over the hot pastry.

**Makes 20**

# hazelnut
## shortbreads

*Photograph page 33*

### ingredients

**1 1/2 cups/185g/6oz flour, sifted**
**45g/1 1/2oz hazelnuts, ground**
**1/4 cup/45g/1 1/2oz ground rice**
**250g/8oz butter, cut into small pieces**
**1/4 cup/60g/2oz caster sugar**
**100g/3 1/2oz chocolate, melted**

**Method:**

1  Place flour, hazelnuts and ground rice in a food processor, add butter and process until mixture resembles coarse bread crumbs. Add sugar and process to combine.

2  Turn mixture onto a floured surface and knead lightly to make a pliable dough. Place dough between sheets of baking paper and roll out to 5mm/1/4in thick. Using a 5cm/2in fluted pastry cutter, cut out rounds of dough and place 3cm/1in apart on greased baking trays. Bake for 20-25 minutes or until lightly browned. Stand on baking trays for 2-3 minutes before transferring to wire racks to cool completely.

3  Place melted chocolate in a plastic food bag, snip off one corner and pipe lines across each biscuit.

Ground hazelnuts give a deliciously different shortbread.

**Makes 40**

**Oven temperature 180°C, 350°F, Gas 4**

# apple
# and blueberry cake

## Method:
1 Place butter, vanilla essence, sugar, eggs, flour and milk in a mixing bowl and beat well until ingredients are combined and mixture is smooth.

2 Spoon half the batter into a greased and lined 20cm/8in round cake tin. Top with half the apple slices and half the blueberries, then remaining batter. Arrange remaining apple and blueberries over top of batter.

3 To make topping, combine sugar and cinnamon and sprinkle over cake. Bake for 55-60 minutes or until cake is cooked when tested with a skewer. Stand in tin for 10 minutes before turning onto a wire rack to cool.

*Variation:* You may like to try replacing the blueberries in this recipe with canned blackberries.

**Makes a 20cm/8in round cake**

## ingredients
125g/4oz  butter, softened
1 teaspoon vanilla essence
$^3/_4$ cup/170g/5$^1/_2$oz caster sugar
2 eggs, lightly beaten
1 $^1/_2$ cups/185g/6oz self-raising flour, sifted
$^1/_2$ cup/125mL/4fl oz buttermilk or milk
220g/7oz canned apple slices
220g/7oz canned blueberries, well drained

### Cinnamon topping
4 teaspoons caster sugar
1 teaspoon ground cinnamon

# thumbprint
## cookies

Photograph page 37

**Method:**

1 *Place butter, icing sugar and vanilla essence in a bowl and beat until light and fluffy. Sift together flour, self-raising flour and custard powder. Fold flour mixture and milk, alternately, into butter mixture.*

2 *Roll tablespoons of mixture into balls and place on greased baking trays. Make a thumbprint in the centre of each cookie.*

3 *Fill thumbprint hole with a teaspoon of jam, lemon curd or chocolate. Bake for 12 minutes or until cookies are golden. Transfer to wire racks to cool.*

**Note:** *Wrap the dough in plastic food wrap and chill at least 30 minutes to make it easier to shape into balls. For a subtle toasty nut flavour, roll the balls in sesame seeds before making the thumbprint and filling.*

**Makes 30**

### ingredients

185g/6oz butter, softened
1/3 cup/45g/1 1/2oz icing sugar, sifted
1 teaspoon vanilla essence
1/2 cup/60g/2oz flour
1 cup/125g/4oz self-raising flour
1/2 cup/60g/2oz custard powder
1/4 cup/60mL/2fl oz milk
jam, lemon curd or chopped chocolate

**Oven temperature 190°C, 375°F, Gas 5**

# monte carlo
## cookies

Photograph page 37

**Method:**

1 *Place butter, brown sugar and vanilla essence in a bowl and beat until light and fluffy. Add egg, flour, self-raising flour, coconut and rolled oats and mix well to combine.*

2 *Roll tablespoons of mixture into balls, place on greased baking trays and flatten slightly with a fork. Bake for 12 minutes or until biscuits are golden. Transfer to wire racks to cool.*

3 *To make Butter Cream, place butter, icing sugar and vanilla essence in a bowl and beat until light and fluffy. Spread half the biscuits with raspberry jam and top with Butter cream. Top with remaining biscuits.*

**Note:** *When shaping the biscuits ensure that all are of uniform size and appearance so that each pair is perfectly matched when sandwiched together.*

**Makes 20**

### ingredients

125g/4oz butter, softened
1 cup/170g/5 1/2oz brown sugar
2 teaspoons vanilla essence
1 egg, lightly beaten
1 cup/125g/4oz flour, sifted
1/2 cup/60g/2oz self-raising flour, sifted
90g/3oz desiccated coconut
3/4 cup/75g/2 1/2oz rolled oats
1/2 cup/155g/5oz raspberry jam
**Butter cream**
60g/2oz butter, softened
1/2 cup/75g/2 1/2oz icing sugar
1 teaspoon vanilla essence

**Oven temperature 190°C, 375°F, Gas 5**

Oven temperature 180°C, 350°F, Gas 4

# spiced
## ginger drops

## Method:
1 Place flour, ground ginger, mixed spice, cinnamon and bicarbonate of soda in a large mixing bowl. Rub in butter until mixture resembles fine bread crumbs. Stir in sugar, golden syrup and glacé ginger.
2 Turn dough onto a lightly floured surface and knead to form a soft dough. Roll rounded teaspoons of mixture into balls and place 3cm/1¼in apart on greased baking trays. Bake for 10-15 minutes or until golden. Transfer biscuits to wire racks to cool.
**Note:** Ginger lovers won't be able to get enough of these spicy cookies.
**Makes 30**

## ingredients

1 cup/125g/4oz flour, sifted
¼ teaspoon ground ginger
¼ teaspoon ground mixed spice
¼ teaspoon ground cinnamon
½ teaspoon bicarbonate of soda
60g/2oz butter, cut into pieces
½ cup/90g/3oz soft brown sugar
2½ tablespoons golden syrup, warmed
1½ tablespoons finely chopped glacé ginger or stem ginger in syrup

# sticky
## carrot and peach cake

**Method:**

1  Sift together flour and bicarbonate of soda into a bowl. Add carrot and peaches and mix to combine. Set aside.
2  Place brown sugar, oil and eggs in a bowl and beat until thick and creamy.
3  Fold egg mixture into flour mixture. Spoon mixture into a greased 23cm/9in round tin and bake for 45 minutes or until cake is cooked when tested with a skewer.
4  To make syrup, place peach juice, sugar, brandy and ginger in a saucepan and heat over a low heat, stirring constantly, until sugar dissolves. Bring syrup to the boil, then reduce heat and simmer for 5 minutes or until slightly thickened.
5  Turn cake onto a serving platter, slowly pour hot syrup over hot cake. Serve hot or warm.

**Makes a 23cm/9in round cake**

### ingredients

1 ½ cups/185g/6oz self-raising flour
1 teaspoon bicarbonate of soda
185g/6oz finely grated raw carrot
440g/14oz canned sliced peaches,
drained and chopped, juice reserved
½ cup/125mL/4fl oz vegetable oil
2 eggs

**Sticky peach syrup**
1 cup/250mL/8fl oz reserved
peach juice
1 cup/250g/8oz sugar
1 tablespoon brandy
½ teaspoon ground ginger

**Oven temperature 180°C, 350°F, Gas 4**

# gingerbread
## men

**Method:**

1 Place butter and sugar in a bowl and beat until light and fluffy. Gradually beat in golden syrup and egg.

2 Sift together flour, ginger, cinnamon and bicarbonate of soda. Add flour mixture to butter mixture and mix to form a soft dough. Divide dough into two portions, wrap in plastic food wrap and refrigerate for 1 hour or until firm.

3 Roll out dough on a lightly floured surface to 5mm/¹/₄in thick. Using a gingerbread man cutter, cut out cookies and place on lightly greased and floured baking trays. Using a small knife and a drinking straw, make indents to form eyes, mouth and buttons. Bake for 10 minutes or until just golden. Stand on trays for 5 minutes before transferring to wire racks to cool.

**Makes 24**

### ingredients

185g/6oz butter, softened
³/₄ cup/125g/4oz brown sugar
¹/₄ cup/90mL/3fl oz golden syrup
1 egg
2³/₄ cups/350g/11oz flour, sifted
2 teaspoons ground ginger
1 teaspoon ground cinnamon
¹/₂ teaspoon bicarbonate of soda

**Oven temperature 180°C, 350°F, Gas 4**

# spicy
## apple cake

## Method:

1 Combine oil and sugar in a large bowl. Whisk in eggs and vanilla. Combine flour and spice in one bowl and apples, lemon rind and sultanas in another. Fold flour mixture and apple mixture alternately into beaten egg mixture.

2 Spoon mixture into a greased and lined 20cm/8in square ring pan and bake at 180°C/350°F/Gas 4 for 30-35 minutes or until cooked. Stand 5 minutes before turning out on a wire rack to cool.

## Serves 12

## ingredients

**3 tablespoons polyunsaturated oil**
**³/₄ cup/190g caster sugar**
**2 eggs, lightly beaten**
**I teaspoon vanilla essence**
**I cup/125g self-raising flour, sifted**
**I¹/₂ teaspoons ground mixed spice**
**410g/13oz canned unsweetened sliced apples, drained**
**I teaspoon grated lemon rind**
**¹/₂ cup/80g sultanas**

# banana nut
## upside-down cake

**Method:**

1 To make topping, place butter and brown sugar in a saucepan and cook over a low heat, stirring constantly, until sugar dissolves and mixture thickens to a syrup.

2 Pour mixture over the base of a greased 23cm/9in round cake tin. Top with banana slices and nuts and set aside.

3 To make cake, place butter and sugar in a bowl and beat until light and fluffy. Gradually beat in eggs.

4 Sift together flour, baking powder and ginger. Fold flour mixture into butter mixture with milk.

5 Spoon mixture over topping in tin and bake for 50 minutes or until cake is cooked when tested with a skewer. Stand cake in tin for 5 minutes before turning out. Serve hot or warm.

**Makes a 23cm/9in round cake**

ingredients

**Nutty topping**
60g/2oz butter
³/₄ cup/125g/4oz brown sugar
3 bananas, sliced lengthwise
100g/3¹/₂oz macadamia or brazil nuts, roughly chopped

**Ginger cake**
100g/3¹/₂oz butter, softened
¹/₂ cup/125g/4oz sugar
2 eggs, lightly beaten
2 cups/250g/8oz flour
1 teaspoon baking powder
1 teaspoon ground ginger
¹/₂ cup/125mL/4fl oz milk

**Oven temperature 180°C, 350°F, Gas 4**

**Oven temperature 180°C, 350°F, Gas 4**

# apricot
## ripple cake

### Method:

1 Place apricots and water in a bowl and set aside to soak for 30 minutes.
2 Place butter and sugar in a bowl and beat until light and fluffy. Gradually beat in eggs.
3 Sift together flour and cinnamon and fold into butter mixture. Spoon half the mixture into a 23cm/9in fluted ring tin.
4 Top mixture with apricots and remaining cake mixture. Bake for 45 minutes or until cake is cooked when tested with a skewer. Stand cake in tin for 5 minutes before turning onto a wire rack to cool.

**Makes a 23cm/9in ring cake**

### ingredients

**125g/4oz dried apricots, chopped
½ cup/125mL/4fl oz hot water
125g/4oz butter, softened
½ cup/125g/4oz sugar
2 eggs, lightly beaten
1½ cups/185g/6oz self-raising flour, sifted
1 teaspoon ground cinnamon**

# raspberry
## truffle cakes

*Photograph page 45*

raspberry truffle cakes

### ingredients

**¹/₂ cup/45g/1¹/₂oz cocoa powder, sifted**
**1 cup/250mL/8fl oz boiling water**
**1³/₄ cups/400g/12¹/₂oz caster sugar**
**125g/4oz butter**
**1¹/₂ tablespoons raspberry jam**
**2 eggs**
**1²/₃ cups/200g/6¹/₂oz self-raising flour, sifted**
**410g/13oz dark chocolate, melted**
**raspberries for garnishing**

**Raspberry cream**
**125g/4oz raspberries, puréed and sieved**
**¹/₂ cup/125mL/4fl oz cream (double), whipped**

**Chocolate sauce**
**125g/4oz dark chocolate**
**¹/₂ cup/125mL/4fl oz water**
**¹/₄ cup/60g/2oz caster sugar**
**1 teaspoon brandy (optional)**

Oven temperature 180°C, 350°F, Gas 4

### Method:

1 Dissolve cocoa powder in boiling water, then cool.

2 Place sugar, butter and jam in a bowl and beat until light and fluffy. Beat in eggs one at a time, adding a little flour with each egg. Fold remaining flour and cocoa mixture, alternately, into butter mixture.

3 Spoon mixture into eight lightly greased ¹/₂ cup/125mL/4fl oz capacity ramekins or large muffin tins. Bake for 20-25 minutes or until cakes are cooked when tested with a skewer. Stand cakes in tins for 5 minutes then turn onto wire racks to cool. Turn cakes upside down and scoop out centre leaving a 1 cm/¹/₂in shell. Spread each cake with chocolate to cover top and sides, then place right way up on a wire rack.

4 To make cream, fold raspberry purée into cream. Spoon cream into a piping bag fitted with a large nozzle. Carefully turn cakes upside down and pipe in cream to fill cavity. Place right way up on individual serving plates.

5 To make sauce, place chocolate and water in a saucepan and cook over a low heat, stirring, for 4-5 minutes or until chocolate melts. Add sugar and continue cooking, stirring constantly, until sugar dissolves. Bring just to the boil, then reduce heat and simmer, stirring, for 2 minutes. Cool for 5 minutes, then stir in brandy, if using. Cool sauce to room temperature and serve with cakes.

**Serves 8**

# ginger
## pear cakes

**Method:**

1 Place sugar, oil, egg and vanilla essence in a bowl and beat to combine. Sift together flour, bicarbonate of soda, ginger and nutmeg. Mix flour mixture into egg mixture, then fold in pears and chopped ginger.

2 Spoon batter into six lightly greased large muffin tins and bake for 20 minutes. Reduce oven temperature to 160°C/325°F/Gas 3 and bake for 15-20 minutes longer, or until cakes are cooked when tested with a skewer.

3 To make Ginger Cream, place cream, sour cream and honey in a bowl and beat until soft peaks form. Add brandy and ground ginger and beat to combine. Fold in chopped ginger. Serve cakes hot or warm accompanied by Ginger cream.

**Serves 6**

## ingredients

¹/₂ cup/125g/4oz raw sugar
¹/₄ cup/60mL/2fl oz vegetable oil
1 egg, lightly beaten
1 teaspoon vanilla essence
1 cup/125g/4oz flour
1 teaspoon bicarbonate of soda
¹/₂ teaspoon ground ginger
¹/₂ teaspoon ground nutmeg
2 pears, cored, peeled and finely diced
155g/5oz glacé ginger or stem ginger in syrup, chopped

### Ginger cream
1 cup/250mL/8fl oz cream (double)
¹/₄ cup/60g/2oz sour cream
1 tablespoon honey
1 tablespoon brandy
¹/₄ teaspoon ground ginger
1 tablespoon finely chopped glacé ginger or stem ginger in syrup

Oven temperature 180°C, 350°F, Gas 4

# flaky
## passion fruit gateau

**Method:**

1  To make filling, place passion fruit pulp, lime juice, butter, eggs and caster sugar in a heatproof bowl set over a saucepan of simmering water and cook, stirring constantly, until mixture thickens. Remove bowl from pan and set aside to cool.

2  On a lightly floured board, roll out pastry to 3mm/¹/₈in thick and cut out three 20cm/8in rounds. Place on lightly greased baking trays, brush with a little milk and sprinkle with sugar. Bake for 12 minutes or until pastry is puffed and golden. Tranfer to wire racks to cool.

3  To assemble gâteau, split pastry rounds in half horizontally. Place one pastry layer on a serving plate, spread with some of the cream and drizzle with some of the filling. Repeat layers, finishing with a layer of cream.

4  Decorate top of gâteau with passion fruit pulp and lime rind strips. Serve immediately.

**Makes a 20cm/8in round cake**

### ingredients

**440g/14oz prepared puff pastry milk**
**2 tablespoons sugar**
**2 cups/500mL/16fl oz cream (double), well chilled and whipped**
**2 tablespoons passion fruit pulp**
**1 tablespoon thin lime rind strips**

**Passion fruit filling**
**¹/₂ cup/125mL/4fl oz passion fruit pulp**
**2 tablespoons lime juice**
**60g/2oz butter**
**2 eggs**
**¹/₃ cup/75g/2¹/₂oz caster sugar**

**Oven temperature 200°C, 400°F, Gas 6**

# fig pinwheel
## cookies

Photograph page 49

fig pinwheel cookies

Oven temperature 180°C. 350°F. Gas 4

### ingredients

170g/5¹/₂oz butter
1 cup/170g/5¹/₂oz soft brown sugar
1 egg
¹/₂ teaspoon vanilla essence
3 cups/375g/12oz flour
¹/₂ teaspoon bicarbonate of soda
¹/₄ teaspoon ground cinnamon
¹/₄ teaspoon ground nutmeg
2 tablespoons milk

**Fig and almond filling**
250g/8oz dried figs, finely chopped
¹/₄ cup/60g/2oz sugar
¹/₂ cup/125ml/4fl oz water
¹/₄ teaspoon ground mixed spice
30g/1oz almonds, finely chopped

## Method:

1 To make filling, place figs, sugar, water and mixed spice in a saucepan and bring to the boil. Reduce heat and cook, stirring, for 2-3 minutes or until mixture is thick. Remove from heat and stir in almonds. Set aside to cool.

2 Place butter in a large mixing bowl and beat until light and fluffy. Gradually add sugar, beating well after each addition until mixture is creamy. Beat in egg and vanilla essence.

3 Sift together flour, bicarbonate of soda, cinnamon and nutmeg. Beat milk and half the flour mixture into butter mixture. Stir in remaining flour mixture. Turn dough onto a lightly floured surface and knead lightly. Roll into a ball, wrap in plastic food wrap and refrigerate for 30 minutes.

4 Divide dough into two portions. Roll one portion out to a 20 x 28cm/8 x 11in rectangle and spread with filling. Roll up from the long side, like a Swiss roll. Repeat with remaining dough and filling. Wrap rolls in plastic food wrap and refrigerate for 15 minutes or until you are ready to cook the biscuits.

5 Cut rolls into 1cm/¹/₂in slices. Place slices on greased baking trays and cook for 10-12 minutes. Stand biscuits on trays for 1 minute before removing to a wire rack to cool completely.

**Freeze it:** The uncooked rolls can be frozen if you wish. When you have unexpected guests or the cookie barrel is empty, these cookies are great standbys.

Pinwheel cookies always look impressive and are very easy to make. Just follow the step-by-step instructions for making these delicious cookies that wrap a spiced dough around a wonderful fig and almond filling.

## Makes 50

*orange and almond gateau*

# citrus flavours

## As an ingredient or decoration,

*the freshly grated zest of oranges, lemons or limes adds a distinctive taste to any cookie, biscuit or slice. Aromatic citrus fruits have found their way into every aspect of cooking - sweet and savoury. Using these delicious recipes fill your tins and jars with unforgettable goodies.*

# orange
## and almond gateau

*Photograph page 51*

**Method:**

1  *To make cake, place caster sugar, eggs, orange juice and rind in a bowl and beat until thick and creamy. Sift together flour, cornflour, baking powder and bicarbonate of soda. Place sour cream and butter in a bowl and whisk lightly to combine. Fold flour and sour cream mixtures, alternately, into egg mixture.*

2  *Spoon batter into three lightly greased and lined 23cm/9in sandwich tins and bake for 15-20 minutes or until cooked when tested with a skewer.*

3  **To make syrup:** *Five minutes before cakes complete cooking, place sugar, orange juice and liqueur in a saucepan and cook over a medium heat, stirring constantly, until sugar dissolves.*

4  *Turn cakes onto wire racks and, using a skewer, pierce surface of cakes to make holes that reach about halfway through the cakes. Spoon hot syrup over hot cakes and cool.*

5  *To make butter cream, place sugar and water in a saucepan and cook over a medium heat, stirring constantly, until sugar dissolves. Bring syrup to the boil and cook until mixture reaches the soft-ball stage (115°C/239°F on a sugar thermometer). Place egg yolks in a bowl, then beat to combine and continue beating while slowly pouring in sugar syrup. Beat for 5 minutes longer or until mixture cools and is of a thick mousse-like consistency. In a separate bowl beat butter until light and creamy, then gradually beat into egg yolk mixture. Beat in orange rind and juice and liqueur.*

6  *To assemble, sandwich cakes together with a little butter cream, then spread remaining butter cream over top and sides of cake. Press almonds around sides of cake.*

**Note:** *The secret to this spectacular cake is to pour the hot sugar syrup over the cooked cakes while they are still hot. Do not pour cold syrup over hot cakes or hot syrup over cold cakes or the cakes will become soggy.*

**Serves 10**

## ingredients

**75g/2¹/₂oz flaked almonds, toasted**

**Sour cream orange cake**
1 cup/220g/7oz caster sugar
3 eggs
4 teaspoons orange juice
1 tablespoon finely grated orange rind
1³/₄ cups/220g/7oz flour
¹/₄ cup/30g/1oz cornflour
1¹/₂ teaspoons baking powder
1 teaspoon bicarbonate of soda
1 cup/250g/8oz sour cream, lightly beaten
250g/8oz butter, melted and cooled

**Orange Syrup**
¹/₂ cup/125g/4oz sugar
¹/₄ cup/60mL/2fl oz orange juice
¹/₄ cup/60mL/2fl oz orange-flavoured liqueur

**Orange butter cream**
¹/₂ cup/125g/4oz sugar
¹/₂ cup/125mL/4fl oz water
4 egg yolks
250g/8oz unsalted butter, softened
2 teaspoons finely grated orange rind
¹/₄ cup/60mL/2fl oz orange juice
2 tablespoons orange-flavoured liqueur

Oven temperature 180°C, 350°F, Gas 4

# easy
## lemon and almond cake

**Method:**

1 Place butter, sugar, lemon butter, eggs, flour, ground almonds and milk in a large mixing bowl and beat well to combine all ingredients.

2 Spoon mixture into a greased and lined 20cm/8in round cake tin and bake for 40 minutes or until cooked when tested with a skewer. Stand cake in tin for 5 minutes before turning onto a wire rack to cool.

3 To make frosting, place cream cheese, lemon rind, icing sugar and lemon juice in a food processor and process for 1 minute or until frosting is of a spreadable consistency. Spread frosting over top of cold cake, then sprinkle with flaked almonds.

**Makes a 20cm/8in round cake**

## ingredients

185g/6oz butter, softened
½ cup/100g/3½oz caster sugar
½ cup/185g/4oz prepared lemon butter (curd)
3 eggs, lightly beaten
1¼ cups/155g/5oz self-raising flour, sifted
30g/1oz ground almonds
½ cup/125mL/4fl oz milk
3 tablespoons flaked almonds, toasted

**<u>Lemon frosting</u>**
125g/4oz cream cheese
1 teaspoon finely grated lemon rind
1½ cups/220g/7oz icing sugar
2 teaspoons lemon juice

**Oven temperature 180°C, 350°F, Gas 4**

# lemon
## syrup cake

### ingredients

**Method:**

1 Place butter, caster sugar and lemon rind in a bowl and beat until light and fluffy. Gradually beat in eggs.

2 Stir flour and coconut into butter mixture. Add sour cream and milk and mix until combined. Spoon mixture into a greased 23 cm/9 in fluted ring tin and bake for 1 hour or until cooked when tested with a skewer.

3 To make syrup, place lemon juice, sugar and water in a saucepan and cook over low heat, stirring constantly, until sugar dissolves. Bring to the boil and simmer for 4 minutes or until syrup thickens slightly.

4 Pour half the hot syrup over the hot cake and stand in tin for 4 minutes. Turn cake onto a serving plate and pour over remaining syrup.

**Makes a 23cm/9in round cake**

125g/4oz butter, softened
1 cup/220g/7oz caster sugar
2 teaspoons finely grated lemon rind
2 eggs, lightly beaten
1 ¹/₂ cups/185g/6oz self-raising flour, sifted
45g/1 ¹/₂oz desiccated coconut
1 ¹/₄ cups/315g/10oz sour cream
¹/₃ cup/90mL/3fl oz milk

**Lemon syrup**
¹/₃ cup/90mL/3fl oz lemon juice
³/₄ cup/185g/6oz sugar
¹/₄ cup/60mL/2fl oz water

**Oven temperature 180°C, 350°F, Gas 4**

**Oven temperature 180°C, 350°F, Gas 4**

# orange
## liqueur layer cake

### Method:

1 *Place eggs in a bowl and beat until thick and creamy. Gradually add sugar, beating well after each addition until mixture is creamy.*

2 *Fold flour and milk into egg mixture. Pour mixture into two greased and lined 26 x 32cm/10¹/₂ x 12³/₄in Swiss roll tins and bake for 10-12 minutes or until cake is cooked. Stand cakes in tins for 5 minutes before turning onto wire racks to cool. Cut each cake into three equal pieces.*

3 *To make filling, place cream, liqueur, icing sugar and orange rind in a bowl and beat until thick.*

4 *To assemble, place a layer of cake on a serving plate and spread with filling. Repeat layers, finishing with a layer of filling. Spread remaining filling over sides of cake and decorate with candied orange peel.*

**Serves 6-8**

### ingredients

**6 eggs**
**1 cup/220g/7oz caster sugar**
**1¹/₂ cups/185g/6oz self-raising flour, sifted**
**¹/₃ cup/90mL/3fl oz warm milk**
**candied orange peel, to decorate**

#### Orange filling

**2 cups/500 mL/16fl oz cream (double)**
**¹/₄ cup/60mL/2fl oz orange-flavoured liqueur**
**2 tablespoons icing sugar**
**2 teaspoons finely grated orange rind**

# orange
## and lime cheesecake

**Method:**

1  Place biscuits and butter in a bowl and mix to combine. Press biscuit mixture over base and up sides of a well-greased 23cm/9in flan tin with a removable base. Bake for 5-8 minutes, then cool.

2  To make filling, place cream cheese, sugar, orange and lime rinds and orange and lime juices in a bowl and beat until creamy. Beat in egg, then mix in condensed milk and fold in cream.

3  Spoon filling into prepared biscuit case and bake for 25-30 minutes or until just firm. Turn oven off and cool cheesecake in oven with door ajar. Chill before serving. Serve cheesecake decorated with toasted coconut.

**Serves 8**

### ingredients

**155g/5oz plain sweet biscuits, crushed**
**90g/3oz butter, melted**
**desiccated coconut, toasted**

**Orange and lime filling**
**185g/6oz cream cheese, softened**
**2 tablespoons brown sugar**
**1¹/₂ teaspoons finely grated orange rind**
**1¹/₂ teaspoons finely grated lime rind**
**3 teaspoons orange juice**
**3 teaspoons lime juice**
**1 egg, lightly beaten**
**¹/₂ cup/125mL/4fl oz sweetened condensed milk**
**2 tablespoons cream (double), whipped**

**Oven temperature 180°C, 350°F, Gas 4**

# lemon
## and pistachio pancakes

**Method:**

1 Place flour and sugar in a bowl and mix to combine. Whisk in yogurt, egg, milk, lemon rind and pistachio nuts and continue whisking until batter is smooth.

2 Cook dessertspoonfuls of mixture in a heated, greased, heavy-based frying pan for 1-2 minutes or until bubbles form on the surface, then turn and cook for 1-2 minutes longer or until golden. Serve immediately.

**Serves 6**

ingredients

1 cup/125g/4oz self-raising flour
¼ cup/60g/2oz sugar
250g/8oz natural yogurt
1 egg, lightly beaten
⅓ cup/90 mL/3fl oz milk
1 tablespoon finely grated lemon rind
60g/2oz chopped pistachio nuts

# choc-chip
## orange cake

**Method:**
1 Place butter, orange rind, sugar, eggs, flour, orange juice, yogurt and milk in a large mixing bowl and beat until all ingredients are combined and batter is smooth. Fold in grated chocolate.
2 Spoon batter into a greased 20cm/8in ring cake tin and bake for 45-50 minutes or until cake is cooked when tested with a skewer. Stand cake in tin for 5 minutes before turning onto a wire rack to cool.
3 To make icing, place butter and orange rind in a mixing bowl and beat until creamy. Add icing sugar, cocoa and orange juice and beat until combined. Add a little more orange juice if necessary. Place in a heatproof bowl over a saucepan of simmering water and cook, stirring constantly, for 2-3 minutes or until mixture is smooth and runny. Pour icing over cold cake.

**Makes a 20cm/8in ring cake**

### ingredients

125g/4oz butter, softened
2 teaspoons grated orange rind
3/4 cup/170g/5 1/2oz caster sugar
2 eggs, lightly beaten
1 1/2 cups/185 g/6 oz self-raising flour, sifted
2 tablespoons freshly squeezed orange juice
1/2 cup/100g/3 1/2oz natural yogurt
1/4 cup/60mL/2fl oz milk
100g/3 1/2oz roughly grated chocolate

**Chocolate icing**
45g/1 1/2oz butter, softened
1/2 teaspoon grated orange rind
3/4 cup/125g/4oz icing sugar, sifted
1 1/2 tablespoons cocoa powder, sifted
4 teaspoons freshly squeezed orange juice

**Oven temperature 180°C, 350°F, Gas 4**

# orange
## poppy seed cake

**Method:**

1 *Combine the poppy seeds and orange juice and allow to stand for 30 minutes.*

2 *Cream together the margarine, sugar, orange rind and vanilla essence, add the eggs one at a time beating well between each addition.*

3 *Fold in the sifted flour, milk and poppy seeds. Spoon mixture into a lightly greased deep 20cm/8in round cake tin. Bake in oven at 180°C/350°F Gas 4 oven for 45-50 minutes, allow to cool in the tin for 5 minutes. When cold ice with orange cream cheese frosting and decorate with candied orange rind.*

4 *To make the Orange Cream Cheese Frosting, beat together softened cream cheese, margarine and orange rind until creamy. Blend in the icing sugar and orange juice and mix well.*

**Serves 8**

### ingredients

¹/₂ **cup poppy seeds**
¹/₂ **cup orange juice**
**125g/4oz margarine**
³/₄ **cup caster sugar**
**grated rind of one orange**
**1 teaspoon vanilla essence**
**2 eggs**
**2 cups self raising flour**
**4 tablespoons milk**

**Orange Cream Cheese Frosting**
**125g/4oz softened cream cheese**
**3 tablespoons margarine**
**grated rind of one orange**
**2 cups sifted icing sugar**
**1 teaspoon orange juice**

Oven temperature 180°C, 350°F, Gas 4

# lemon
## yoghurt cake

### Method:

1  Place butter, sugar, lemon rind and vanilla essence in a bowl and beat until light and creamy. Add eggs one at a time, beating well after each addition.

2  Add flour, lemon juice and yogurt and mix to combine. Pour batter into a greased 23cm/9in fluted ring tin and bake for 1 hour or until cake is cooked when tested with a skewer.

3  To make syrup, place sugar and lemon juice in a saucepan and cook over a low heat, stirring constantly, until sugar dissolves. Bring to the boil and cook, without stirring, for 4 minutes or until mixture thickens slightly. Pour hot syrup over hot cake in tin. Stand for 5 minutes before turning onto a serving plate.

### ingredients

185g/6oz butter
³/₄ cup/185g/6oz sugar
1 tablespoon finely grated lemon rind
1 teaspoon vanilla essence
2 eggs, lightly beaten
2¹/₄ cups/280g/9oz self-raising flour, sifted
¹/₄ cup/60mL/2fl oz lemon juice
1 cup/200g/6¹/₄oz natural yogurt

**Lemon syrup**
1 cup/250g/8oz sugar
¹/₂ cup/125 mL/4fl oz lemon juice

Oven temperature 190°C, 375°F, Gas 5

# lemon
## marshmallow slice

### Method:

1 Place crushed cookies, butter and coconut in a bowl and mix well to combine. Press mixture into a greased and lined shallow 18 x 28cm/ 7 x 11in cake tin. Refrigerate until firm.

2 To make filling, place marshmallows, gelatine, milk, lemon juice and rind in a saucepan and cook, stirring, over a low heat until mixture is smooth and gelatine dissolves. Remove from heat and allow to cool, stirring every 3-5 minutes. Pour over biscuit base and refrigerate until firm.

*Lime Marshmallow Slice:* Replace lemon juice and rind with lime juice and rind.

*Note:* A fluffy marshmallow topping combines with a crunchy coconut base to make this delicious no-bake slice.

**Makes 30**

### ingredients

**100g/3¹/₂oz plain sweet cookies, crushed
60g/2oz butter, melted
30g/1oz desiccated coconut**

**Lemon Marshmallows toppings
400g/9¹/₂oz white marshmallows
4 teaspoons gelatine
²/₃ cup/170mL/5¹/₂fl oz milk
¹/₃ cup/90mL/3fl oz lemon juice
¹/₂ cup/90g/3oz finely grated lemon rind**

*ham and mustard scrolls*

# something savoury

## Who could resist a slice of savoury

*bread fresh from the oven? These recipes make perfect accompaniments for soups and salads, as well as being tasty meals on their own,*

# mexican
## cornbread

*Photograph page 63*

### Method:

1  *Place cornmeal (polenta), flour, tasty cheese (mature Cheddar), Parmesan cheese, olives, sun-dried tomatoes, sweet corn and green peppers in a bowl and mix to combine.*
2  *Combine eggs, milk, yogurt and oil. Add egg mixture to dry ingredients and mix until just combined.*
3  *Pour mixture into a greased 20cm/8in springform pan and bake for 1 hour or until bread is cooked when tested with a skewer. Serve warm or cold.*

**Makes a 20cm/8in round loaf**

### ingredients

**2 cups/350g/11oz cornmeal (polenta)
2 cups/250g/8oz self-raising flour, sifted
125g/4oz grated tasty cheese
(mature Cheddar)
60g/2oz grated Parmesan cheese
12 pitted black olives, sliced
12 sun-dried tomatoes, chopped
100g/3¹/₂oz canned sweet corn kernels,
drained
3 bottled hot green peppers,
chopped finely
2 eggs, lightly beaten
1 cup/250mL/8fl oz milk
³/₄ cup/155g/5oz yogurt
¹/₄ cup/60mL/2fl oz vegetable oil**

# ham
## and mustard scrolls

*Photograph page 63*

### Method:

1  *Place flour, baking powder and butter in a food processor and process until mixture resembles coarse breadcrumbs. With machine running, slowly add egg and milk and process to form a soft dough. Turn dough onto a lightly floured surface and press out to make a 1cm/¹/₂in thick rectangle.*
2  *To make filling, place ham, ricotta cheese, tasty cheese (mature Cheddar) and mustard into a bowl and mix to combine. Spread filling over dough and roll up from short side.*
3  *Using a serrated edged knife, cut roll into 2cm/³/₄in thick slices and place on a lightly greased and floured baking tray. Bake for 15-20 minutes or until puffed and golden.*

**Makes 18**

### ingredients

**2 cups/250g/8oz self-raising flour, sifted
1 teaspoon baking powder, sifted
60g/2oz butter, chopped
1 egg, lightly beaten
¹/₂ cup/125mL/4fl oz milk**

**Ham and mustard filling**
**4 slices smoked ham, chopped
¹/₂ cup/125g/4oz ricotta cheese, drained
60g/2oz grated tasty cheese
(mature Cheddar)
2 tablespoons wholegrain mustard**

# potato
## and cheese pancake

### Method:

1 Rinse potatoes in a colander under cold running water, then turn onto a clean teatowel or absorbent kitchen paper and pat dry.

2 Place potatoes, eggs, onions, flour, coriander, Cheddar cheese and black pepper to taste in a bowl and mix to combine.

3 Heat oil in a large nonstick frying pan over a medium heat, spread potato mixture over base of pan and cook for 15 minutes. Place pan under a preheated medium grill and cook for 10 minutes or until top is golden and pancake is cooked through. Serve cut into wedges and topped with yoghurt.

**Serves 6-8**

### ingredients

1 kg/2 lb potatoes, grated
2 eggs, lightly beaten
2 onions, grated
2 tablespoons flour
1 teaspoon finely chopped fresh coriander
60g/2oz reduced-fat Cheddar cheese, grated
freshly ground black pepper
2 tablespoons olive oil
6 tablespoons low-fat natural yogurt

# basil
## beer bread

*Photograph page 67*

### ingredients

**3 cups/375g/12oz self-raising flour, sifted**
**¹/₄ cup/60g/2oz sugar**
**6 tablespoons chopped fresh basil**
**1 teaspoon crushed black peppercorns**
**1¹/₂ cups/375mL/12fl oz beer, at room temperature**

**Method:**
1 *Place flour, sugar, basil, peppercorns and beer in a bowl and mix to make a soft dough.*
2 *Place dough in a greased and lined 11x21cm/ 4¹/₂ x 8¹/₂in loaf tin and bake for 50 minutes or until bread is cooked when tested with a skewer.*
3 *Stand bread in tin for 5 minutes before turning onto a wire rack to cool. Serve warm or cold.*
**Makes an 11x 21cm/4¹/₂x8¹/₂in loaf**

# olive
## soda bread

*Photograph page 67*

### ingredients

**125g/4oz butter, softened**
**¹/₄ cup/60g/2oz sugar**
**1 egg**
**3 cups/470g/15oz wholemeal self-raising flour**
**1¹/₂ cups/185g/6oz flour**
**1¹/₂ teaspoons bicarbonate of soda**
**1¹/₂ cups/375mL/12fl oz buttermilk or milk**
**125g/4oz black olives, chopped**
**2 teaspoons fennel seeds**
**1 teaspoon coarse sea salt**

**Method:**
1 *Place butter, sugar and egg in a food processor and process until smooth. Add wholemeal flour, flour, bicarbonate of soda and milk and process to form a soft dough.*
2 *Turn dough onto a lightly floured surface and knead in olives. Shape dough into a 20cm/8in round and place on a lightly greased and floured baking tray. Using a sharp knife, cut a cross in the top. Sprinkle with fennel seeds and salt and bake for 45 minutes or until cooked.*
**Makes a 20cm/8in round loaf**

Oven temperature 160°C, 325°F, Gas 3

Oven temperature 200°C, 400°F, Gas 6

*rock cakes and carrot cake*

# healthy alternative

**Good tastes that are full of goodness**

*Enjoy these cakes, cookies and slices anytime of the day for snacks or treats.*

# rock
## cakes

*Photograph page 69*

### ingredients

**2 cups/250g/8oz self-raising flour, sifted**
**¼ cup/60g/2oz caster sugar**
**90g/3oz butter**
**125g/4oz mixed dried fruit, chopped**
**1 teaspoon finely grated lemon rind**
**1 teaspoon finely grated orange rind**
**1 egg, lightly beaten**
**⅓ cup/90mL/3fl oz milk**
**½ teaspoon cinnamon mixed with**
**2 tablespoons caster sugar**

**Method:**
1 *Place flour and sugar in a mixing bowl. Rub in butter, using fingertips, until mixture resembles fine bread crumbs. Stir in mixed fruit, lemon rind and orange rind. Add egg and milk and mix to form a soft dough.*
2 *Place tablespoons of mixture on greased baking trays and dust lightly with cinnamon sugar mixture. Bake for 12-15 minutes or until golden. Transfer to wire racks to cool.*
**Makes 30**

---

# carrot
## cake

*Photograph page 69*

### ingredients

**2 cups/375g/2oz ground rice, sifted**
**2 teaspoons ground mixed spice**
**2 teaspoons bicarbonate of soda**
**1 cup/170g/5½oz soft brown sugar**
**125g/4oz margarine, softened**
**4 small carrots, grated**
**125g/4oz pecans, chopped**
**170g/5½oz sultanas**
**2 cups/400g/12½oz natural low-fat yogurt**
**1 teaspoon vanilla essence**
**icing sugar**

**Method:**
1 *Place ground rice, mixed spice, bicarbonate of soda, brown sugar, margarine, carrots, pecans, sultanas, yogurt and vanilla essence in a large mixing bowl and mix well to combine all ingredients.*
2 *Spoon mixture into a greased and lined 20 cm/8 in square cake tin and bake for 45-50 minutes or until cooked when tested with a skewer. Stand cake in tin for 10 minutes before turning onto a wire rack to cool. Dust with icing sugar.*
**Note:** *A gluten-free cake that is suitable for anyone who has a wheat intolerance.*
**Makes a 20cm/8in square cake**

healthy
alternative

**Oven temperature 190°C, 375°F, Gas 5**

# apricot
## date slice

### Method:

1  Place apricots in a small bowl and add boiling water to cover. Set aside to soak for 10 minutes. Drain.

2  Sift together flour and sugar into a large mixing bowl. Add coconut, dates and apricots, pour in melted butter and mix to combine. Press mixture into a greased and lined, shallow 18 x 28cm/7 x 11in cake tin and bake for 25 minutes or until firm. Allow to cool in tin.

3  To make icing, place butter in a mixing bowl and beat until creamy. Add icing sugar and lemon juice and beat until icing is of a spreadable consistency. Add a little more lemon juice if necessary.

**Note:** Spread icing over cold slice and sprinkle with coconut. Cut into bars.

**Makes 30**

### ingredients

90g/3oz dried apricots, chopped
boiling water
2 cups/250g/8oz self-raising flour, sifted
1 cup/170g/5¹/₂oz soft brown sugar
75g/2¹/₂oz desiccated coconut
60g/2oz dates, chopped
185g/6oz butter, melted

#### Lemon icing
90g/3oz butter, softened
1¹/₂ cups/220g/7oz icing sugar, sifted
2 tablespoons lemon juice
15g/¹/₂oz desiccated coconut, toasted

# pineapple
## and museli cookies

**Method:**
1  *Place muesli, flour, sugar and pineapple in a bowl. Add butter and egg and mix well to combine.*
2  *Place spoonfuls of mixture on greased baking trays and bake for 12-15 minutes or until golden brown. Stand on trays for 5 minutes before removing to wire racks to cool.*
**Makes 30**

ingredients

2 cups/250g/8oz toasted muesli
1 cup/125g/4oz self-raising flour, sifted
¹/₂ cup/125g/4oz demerara sugar
45g/1¹/₂oz glacé pineapple, chopped
125g/4oz butter, melted
1 egg, lightly beaten

**Oven temperature 180°C, 350°F, Gas 4**

Oven temperature 180°C, 350°F, Gas 4

# honey
## oat loaf

### Method:

1 Sift together flour and self-raising flour, salt and baking powder into a large mixing bowl. Stir in rolled oats.

2 Combine butter, eggs, water and honey and mix into flour mixture until just combined. Pour into a greased and lined 11 x 21cm/ 4¹/₂ x 8¹/₂in loaf tin and bake for 40-45 minutes or until cooked when tested with a skewer. Stand in tin for 5 minutes before turning onto a wire rack to cool completely. Plain, or spread with a little butter and jam, this loaf tastes delicious.

**Makes an 11 x 21cm/
4¹/₂x8¹/₂in loaf**

### ingredients

¹/₂ cup/60g/2oz flour
1 cup/125g/4oz self-raising flour
1 teaspoon salt
1¹/₂ teaspoons baking powder
1 cup/90g/3oz rolled oats
45g/1¹/₂oz butter, melted
2 eggs, lightly beaten
¹/₄ cup/60mL/2fl oz water
¹/₂ cup/170g/5¹/₂oz honey, warmed

# fruity
## cereal slice

Photograph page 75

**Method:**

1 Place rice cereal, bran flakes, almonds, apricots, pineapple, ginger, raisins and sultanas in a large mixing bowl and set aside.

2 Combine butter, cream, honey and sugar in a saucepan and cook over a low heat, stirring constantly, until sugar dissolves and butter melts. Bring to the boil, then reduce heat and simmer for 5 minutes or until mixture thickens slightly.

3 Pour honey mixture into dry ingredients and mix well to combine. Press mixture into a greased and lined shallow 18x28cm/ 7x11in cake tin. Refrigerate until firm, then cut into squares.

**Note:** Dried fruit, rice bubbles, coconut, nuts and honey – just reading the ingredients you know that this slice is going to be delicious.

**Makes 30**

### ingredients

**3 cups/90g/3oz unsweetened puffed rice cereal
1 cup/45g/1½oz bran flakes, crumbled
125g/4oz slivered almonds, toasted
125g/4oz dried apricots, chopped
100g/3½oz glacé pineapple, chopped
100g/3½oz glacé ginger or stem ginger in syrup, chopped
90g/3oz raisins, chopped
170g/5½oz sultanas
125g/4oz butter
½ cup/125mL/4fl oz cream (double)
½ cup/170g/5½oz honey
⅓ cup/90g/3oz demerara sugar**

# date bars

Photograph page 75

**Method:**

1 Place evaporated milk in a saucepan and cook over a low heat until just boiling, then remove pan from heat. Place dates in a bowl, pour hot milk over and set aside to cool.

2 Combine butter, sugar and vanilla essence in a large mixing bowl and beat until light and fluffy. Mix flour and date mixture, alternately, into butter mixture, then fold in pecans. Spoon mixture into a greased and lined 23cm/9in square cake tin and bake for 25-30 minutes or until firm. Stand in tin 5 minutes before turning onto a wire rack to cool. Cut into bars.

**Note:** Studded with dates and pecans, this slice is a great lunch box filler.

**Makes 30**

### ingredients

**¾ cup/185mL/6fl oz evaporated milk
125g/4oz pitted dates, chopped
125g/4oz butter, softened
½ cup/100g/3½oz caster sugar
1 teaspoon vanilla essence
1 cup/125g/4oz self-raising flour, sifted
60g/2oz pecans, chopped**

Oven temperature 180°C, 350°F, Gas 4

# icing
## on the cake

### The icing on the cake

*This selection of easy icings, fillings and toppings will dress up any plain cake to make it into something really special.*

### Chocolate ripple cream

*Cream well chilled, with chocolate folded through as soon as it is melted - the secret to this wonderful topping or filling for a chocolate cake or sponge.*

*Enough to fill and top a 20cm/8in cake*

**100g/3¹/₂oz dark chocolate**
**1 cup/250mL/8fl oz cream (double),**
**well chilled and whipped**

*Melt chocolate in a small bowl over a saucepan of simmering water, or melt in the microwave oven on HIGH (100%) for 45 seconds to 1 minute. Fold melted chocolate through chilled cream.*

### Butterscotch frosting

*Enough to cover a 20cm/8in cake*

**1¹/₂ cups/250g/8oz soft brown sugar**
**¹/₄ cup/60mL/2fl oz milk**
**30g/1oz butter**
**1 cup/155g/5oz icing sugar**

*Place sugar, milk and butter in a small saucepan and cook, stirring constantly, over a low heat until sugar dissolves. Bring to the boil and boil for 3-4 minutes. Remove from heat and set aside to cool until just warm, then beat in icing sugar until frosting is of a spreadable consistency. Use immediately.*

### Vanilla butter icing

*Enough to cover a 20cm/8in cake or 18 biscuits*

**1¹/₂ cups/220g/7oz icing sugar, sifted**
**60g/2oz butter**
**2 tablespoons boiling water**
**¹/₄ teaspoon vanilla essence**
**few drops of food colouring (optional)**

*Place icing sugar and butter in a bowl and add boiling water. Mix to make a mixture of spreadable consistency, adding a little more water if necessary. Beat in vanilla essence and food colouring if using.*

### Chocolate Butter Icing

*Add ¹/₄ cup/30g/1oz cocoa powder to icing sugar.*

### Coffee Butter Icing:

*Add 1 tablespoon instant coffee powder to boiling water.*

### Lemon Butter Icing:

*Omit vanilla essence and add 1-2 teaspoons fresh lemon juice to icing sugar mixture.*

### Passion Fruit Icing:

*Replace vanilla essence with 2-3 tablespoons passion fruit pulp. A little more icing sugar may be required to make an icing of spreadable consistency.*

# icing
## on the cake

### Mock cream

*Enough to fill a 20cm/8in cake*

**60g/2oz butter**

**¼ cup/60g/2oz caster sugar**

**¼ cup/60mL/2fl oz boiling water**

**¼ teaspoon vanilla essence**

*Place butter and sugar in a small bowl and add boiling water. Beat, using an electric mixer, until creamy. Beat in vanilla essence.*

*Cook's tip: If the mixture curdles, place over a pan of simmering water and continue beating.*

### Chocolate fudge topping

*Enough to fill and cover a 20cm/8in cake*

**¾ cup/185g/6oz caster sugar**

**⅓ cup/90mL/3fl oz evaporated milk**

**125g/4oz dark chocolate,**
**broken into pieces**

**45g/1½oz butter**

**¼ teaspoon vanilla essence**

**1** *Place sugar and evaporated milk in a heavy-based saucepan and cook, stirring, over a low heat until sugar melts. Bring mixture to the boil and simmer stirring constantly for 4 minutes.*

**2** *Remove pan from heat and stir in chocolate. Continue stirring until chocolate melts, then stir in butter and vanilla essence.*

**3** *Transfer frosting to a bowl and set aside to cool. Cover with plastic food wrap and chill until frosting thickens and is of spreadable consistency.*

### Marshmallow frosting

*Enough to fill and cover a 20cm/8in cake*

**1 egg white**

**2 teaspoons gelatine dissolved in**

**½ cup/125mL/4fl oz hot water, cooled**

**1 cup/155g/5oz icing sugar**

**flavouring of your choice**

**few drops of colouring (optional)**

*Beat egg white until stiff peaks form, then continue beating while gradually adding gelatine mixture. Beat in icing sugar and flavouring. Continue beating until frosting is thick.*

Cooking is not an exact science: one does not require finely calibrated scales, pipettes and scientific equipment to cook, yet the conversion to metric measures in some countries and its interpretations must have intimidated many a good cook.

Weights are given in the recipes only for ingredients such as meats, fish, poultry and some vegetables. Though a few grams/ounces one way or another will not affect the success of your dish.

Though recipes have been tested using the Australian Standard 250mL cup, 20mL tablespoon and 5mL teaspoon, they will work just as well with the US and Canadian 8fl oz cup, or the UK 300mL cup. We have used graduated cup measures in preference to tablespoon measures so that proportions are always the same. Where tablespoon measures have been given, these are not crucial measures, so using the smaller tablespoon of the US or UK will not affect the recipe's success. At least we all agree on the teaspoon size.

For breads, cakes and pastries, the only area which might cause concern is where eggs are used, as proportions will then vary. If working with a 250mL or 300mL cup, use large eggs (60g/2oz), adding a little more liquid to the recipe for 300mL cup measures if it seems necessary. Use the medium-sized eggs (55g/1$^{1}$/$_{4}$oz) with 8fl oz cup measure. A graduated set of measuring cups and spoons is recommended, the cups in particular for measuring dry ingredients. Remember to level such ingredients to ensure their accuracy.

### English measures

All measurements are similar to Australian with two exceptions: the English cup measures 300mL/10fl oz, whereas the Australian cup measure 250mL/8fl oz. The English tablespoon (the Australian dessertspoon) measures 14.8mL/$^{1}$/$_{2}$fl oz against the Australian tablespoon of 20mL/$^{3}$/$_{4}$fl oz.

### American measures

The American reputed pint is 16fl oz, a quart is equal to 32fl oz and the American gallon, 128fl oz. The Imperial measurement is 20fl oz to the pint, 40fl oz a quart and 160fl oz one gallon.

The American tablespoon is equal to 14.8mL/$^{1}$/$_{2}$fl oz, the teaspoon is 5mL/$^{1}$/$_{6}$fl oz. The cup measure is 250mL/8fl oz, the same as Australia.

### Dry measures

All the measures are level, so when you have filled a cup or spoon, level it off with the edge of a knife. The scale below is the "cook's equivalent"; it is not an exact conversion of metric to imperial measurement. To calculate the exact metric equivalent yourself, use 2.2046 lb = 1kg or 1 lb = 0.45359kg

| Metric | | Imperial | |
|---|---|---|---|
| g = grams | | oz = ounces | |
| kg = kilograms | | lb = pound | |
| 15g | | $^{1}$/$_{2}$oz | |
| 20g | | $^{2}$/$_{3}$oz | |
| 30g | | 1oz | |
| 60g | | 2oz | |
| 90g | | 3oz | |
| 125g | | 4oz | $^{1}$/$_{4}$ lb |
| 155g | | 5oz | |
| 185g | | 6oz | |
| 220g | | 7oz | |
| 250g | | 8oz | $^{1}$/$_{2}$ lb |
| 280g | | 9oz | |
| 315g | | 10oz | |
| 345g | | 11oz | |
| 375g | | 12oz | $^{3}$/$_{4}$ lb |
| 410g | | 13oz | |
| 440g | | 14oz | |
| 470g | | 15oz | |
| 1,000g | 1kg | 35.2oz | 2.2 lb |
| | 1.5kg | | 3.3 lb |

### Oven temperatures

The Celsius temperatures given here are not exact; they have been rounded off and are given as a guide only. Follow the manufacturer's temperature guide, relating it to oven description given in the recipe. Remember gas ovens are hottest at the top, electric ovens at the bottom and convection-fan forced ovens are usually even throughout. We included Regulo numbers for gas cookers which may assist. To convert °C to °F multiply °C by 9 and divide by 5 then add 32.